Wintergreen

Wintergreen

CHARLES BENNETT

HEADLAND

First published in 2002
by
HEADLAND PUBLICATIONS
38 York Avenue, West Kirby,
Wirral CH48 3JF

British Library Cataloguing in Publication Data.
A full CIP record for this book is available from the British Library

ISBN: 1 902096 74 6

HEADLAND acknowledges the financial
assistance of North West Arts Board

Printed in Great Britain by
L. Cocker & Co., Berry Street, Liverpool

To Phillippa,
who put the word *wife* in my mouth

CONTENTS

LOST

Wintergreen

Sprinkles of snow in the spruce woods,
night-lights that ripple and whisper

in thickets of larch and pine.
In the axils of upper leaves

your white star-like corolla
a soothment for wounds.

You are good for clarity of mind –
repeating your name at night

in periods of drought
renders the spirit receptive.

Somewhere close at hand
you are hiding until I find you:

a remedy for solitude
a prickle of white in the wood.

The Unicorn Diaries

I put you together from pentagrams of sugar
and salt, from the bones of eleven mice.

I wondered at first if the smell was viburnum
or phosphorus, if the feathers

were swans or doves, if the dimpled sheets
of your bed, were the toad's pale underbelly,

or fallen hawthorn blossom. Then
when I found the diaries I knew

why you slowly dismembered a wedding dress
into shreds of soft confetti. What was it like

that night? I found the window open, the bath
still full of milk, hoof-prints in the snow.

Only Her Lips Remember

When it snows her birthmarks return –
a thumbprint opens on her throat
and suddenly she's blushed
with a comet's tail, a leaping hare:
familiar bilberry islands, twelve
strange shapes I recognise
but do not understand.

She ties white ribbon on the damson,
drinks nothing but milk, tells me
again (strawberry clouds
clotting her skin) not to go out.
It happens overnight – by the time
I wake from a dream of seventeen skylarks
she is smiling at the rain.

Teeth

At night they hoist their peppermint sails
and slip from harbour one by one

to become whatever takes their eye:
an opal cat who pours like milk

beneath the glow of china roses,
a cabbage white which flitters

like smithereens of snow,
flakes of torn-up letters

in a whirl of hanging clauses.
You've probably seen one:

a blonde in ivory satin, a stranded
car like a single pearl cool and alone

in the all-night car-park, an albino bathtub
luscious as a slice of vanilla ice-cream...

A swan on the purple river
stretches its eggshell wings,

overhead the squonk of a goose
announces the end of night.

And now my bedraggled sheep come home,
a choir of ruffled clouds

trying to remember their order,
innocent as an empty sheet of paper.

As long as I live they'll wander each night
into the world; but once I'm dead

they'll stay where they are
like stars that show you how things were.

The Saltings

Towards the end of afternoons
when light is almost over

a trickle of shadow licks
the filament of tributaries

wrinkled cracks and crevices
which only a moment ago were dry

now with dross and flotsam clog
and swell – nightfall waters

seep like sap, saltwort
and shrubby seablight breathe

and everything stands on tiptoe until
a yellow moon comes in with the tide

and then the saltings are flooded fields
of meadow-sweet and marigold.

Agrimony

The sting of lemon in your kiss
draws bitterness from a wound

unravels dreams and eases
whatever is out of joint

in thickets and all waste places.
Spikes of yellow flowers

acrid at the edges of meadows
and a small, sweet-scented root

are a mild astringent and tonic
for such as are bitten by serpents.

Soft and slightly aromatic
your much-cut-into leaves

downy above and more densely so beneath
have the power of putting to sleep

the man who lays you beneath his head
with the scent of crab-apple, apricot, quince.

Nothing

I'm watching a wren
flicker round the branches
of the crab-apple tree
in our back garden.

Next door but one
spent most of the morning
ticking off his roses
with a pair of secateurs.

At the end of his garden
a bonfire smoulders
from the bottom of a galvanised dustbin.
Nothing is happening

just at the moment
which is fine by me –
the blossom will come
when it's ready,

sooner or later
the fruit will be home.
The smoke has its own sour music
to which a ginger cat

is listening. Meanwhile
the wren goes flittering
round each of the naked branches
in no particular order.

Zanzibar

In the tree house my father never made,
I discovered French jazz while learning to swim
from diagrams. With a dirge composed in advance,
played on a plastic harmonica, I mourned
the ladybird kept in a matchbox and fed
on darkness. The woman who drank the blood
of cats turned into a swan. At night
the poison ice-cream van tinkled ever closer.
I made gallimaufry, wore galligaskins,
smiled at the moon. After his murder
my father's organs dangled in seventeen
shoeboxes. At Zanzibar I understood
the nature of bras and knickers
in the Universal Catalogue. In Constantinople
I dawdled my first cigarette. The canopy
was an old green tent. It smelt of resin
and creosote. When the radio died
I slung it beneath some yellow balloons,
used it as bait for vultures.

The November Piano

For each of the notes you bring to light –
dipping your fingers into this
and whatever comes next,
allowing the touches to last
for just so long – a leaf
on the tree in our garden
is taken by the wind.

By the time it's dark I will
know quite well how it goes,
how the first few drops of rain
on the final afternoon of November
are only to be expected, how
something begins when a tree
is undressed by a song.

The Storm Bell

It pelted on the Thursday I was made.
The men drank tea and the sparrows bickered
in the roof of the shed. On Freehold Street
generations of groundsel, ragwort, flea-bane
fizzled beneath a graphite sky.

I was nothing but a shell of empty air,
a billowing spinnaker eager for the bloom
of molten breath. As lightning snapped
they gave me life in a plunge of flame
and filled me full of thunder.

From the door of my wholly open mouth
I release a single vowel
supple as the willow which purifies metal
it trembles with the chirm of a storm
and gleams like the flowers on Freehold Street.

The Mermaid Room

My room is like the inside of an oyster shell –
at high tide the water reaches halfway up the wall,
the door can be opened without spilling a drop.

My treasures are a toast-rack and an eggcup,
a pair of stilettos, a little black dress
and twenty-seven wedding rings.

On foggy nights I am the melancholy
smooch of a saxophone, leading you astray.
In summer, flute-laughter shivers from my throat.

You find me one evening in autumn
following the hint of lemon-grass and cinnamon
that lead up the stairs to a numbered door.

I am sunlight on the under-floor of forest,
cardamon, galangal, ginger –
a soft commingling of constellations;

I am the voyage you will make alone
in a small, unstable, open boat
for the rest of your life...

In the morning they'll find you in the harbour
your lungs full of daisies and snails in your hair,
traces of gold beneath your nails.

The fishermen will shake their heads:
they've seen that rapturous, troubled look
too many times.

By then, I'll have had my breakfast
my face will be flickering like faces in a dream
or a water-colour, overcome with rain.

William Wordsworth's Socks

As if a single drop of rain
from all the deep protracted rush

which smashed the mere
to a miserable blur

had been preserved – I found,
nestled at the end of memory

like a pair of inverted commas
closing a lively correspondence

of which nothing else remained,
your old grey socks;

quiet and tidy and labelled
with a set of neat initials

they waited patiently as dogs:
watching the rain with one eye open

wanting to go for a walk.

The Library of Rain

It was utterly wonderful to me to find that I could go so heartily and headily
mad; for you know I had been priding myself on my peculiar sanity!

John Ruskin. Letter to Thomas Carlyle, 23 June 1878

I stand at the bottom of Coniston,
    deep in a meadow
of ancient leaves – swart and sallow,
    fuliginous, deciduous,
up to my knees where the autumns
    of England are kept
undercover. This is how the rocks begin:
    my house is made of days –
those stones were leaves which dandled in the sun,
    my house is a mausoleum.

Light drifts down through the water,
    as if it were heavy:
grains of light, like seeds in the swell,
    golden motes of pollen,
tranquil as sun-inflected cirrus,
    fall through the dark;
eggs of light – magnesium and mercury,
    opal sparks of fireworks
swirling in waves of amethyst
    and amber.

I am deep in the wisdom of water,
          do not disturb me:
evaporation – condensation – precipitation;
          I am falling
with the rain on Coniston water,
          where each of the streams
from How Head to Lake Bank
          has its own voice:
alone in the library of rain, I listen
          to cadence and nuance.

Soaked to the skin with fallen light,
          I am comfortable here.
In time I expect to resemble
          the gudgeon, tench and barbel
snuffling through what appears at first
          wholly unremarkable.
Will it matter if I go unremembered,
          if nothing was done?
I leave my work to do itself,
          lucent as rain in autumn.

Swarm Haugh Closes

Hereward the Wake survived by becoming virtually invisible. From
his hideout in the reed-beds and marshes he lived up to his
nickname by remaining watchful, alert and always more awake than
his contemporaries. It was perfectly fitting and natural then, that
after the siege of Ely (1071) Hereward disappeared into the
surrounding countryside. His whereabouts remained unknown, his
history untraceable, from then on. His final resting-place is a
complete mystery.

1

My finger-bones are willow leaves –
at Witcham Hythe and Soham Cotes
they play the notes of ditch and dyke.

The music of England is acorns and apples
puddles underfoot and showers overhead
primrose and cowslip and Jack-by-the-hedge.

Over this land which is neither field
nor flowing stream, the rain-clouds send
their swart, continual symphony.

Sloes are moments of thunder
and rose-hips hold the sunset
as the end of October trembles

in the levels of Coveney Sedge.

2

My tongue is nimble as the speckled newt:
I speak in accents of meadow-sweet

and duckweed, my vowels are thickened
with sticklebacks and water-cress:

rain is my love-song to the land.
When evensong settles on Frogs Abbey

I add my voice to the clotted psalms
of olive and yellow nightingales

who gargle at the stars.
My words have webbed feet.

Soon you will hear what I have to say:
my voice is the stipple of rain on leaves

the drip of a tap in the middle of the night
the slish of a car beneath your window

drizzle on Haddenham Pastures.

3

The lane that dawdles round Wardy Hill
where grasses lisp their simple names
is following the outline of my ear.

I am listening to a cloud's pale melody,
to the moor-hen's chick as it scrapes
at the sky of its egg.

I hear beyond the brittle thrum
and twang of your excited heart
as autumn begins:

a tatty crow from Sutton Gault
grinds his ruined cello
and sunlight, smashed apart

is drowned in Somersham Meadow.

4

My spine is a straggle of hollows
the track at Wenny Severals

a ditch where the keel of a village
rested by the hedge

and the ridge of a disused railway
disguised by elder and alder.

The stations of my vertebrae
are a stubble of knolls and tumps

where blackbirds release their songs
from one to the other.

I am watchful still:
when raindrops shatter with moonlight

a yellow trail of tormentil
finds its way to where you are

from the quiet copse on Loveden Hill.

5

A trickle of water from Tholomas Drove
filters through the hollow of my skull
and wriggles like thought.

From an outcrop of reeds I keep my watch.
I have drowned the determined, confident plough
in a wallow of softness.

Where the road curves round from Outwell to Upwell
in a push of mirrors and screens
I recover the meaning of *wind* and *wing*.

I am the gaze of the heron
counting the glint of minnows.
I am the shoal of memories

in the mind of Swarm Haugh Closes.

Nettle

First of the flowers I knew
to avoid, at thirteen I ran

stark-naked through the wood
and fell into your embrace.

You have made from yourself
this shirt I wear, sheets for our bed

a square of paper. I must pluck you
by the roots if ever I wish to be cured

plant you in rows by the beehive
to drive away frogs

drizzle you softly across my tongue
to remember our first night together.

Thetis

Although the smell of this matchbox
sandpaper reddened with sulphur

brings me your sunburnt face
and your smile as I light one because

today is your birthday and so
is tomorrow and whenever

we close our eyes to sniff
the blown-out candles while

kissing each other's cheeks,
the keepsake ring you gave me

on condition I'd wear it always
is glinting at the bottom of a rock-pool.

Sisal

What happened to the knots I used to know,
the sheep-shank, reef knot, granny? I'd show
you how they went, how the rabbit
came out of his burrow, ran once round the tree
and then... I was tying myself to nothing.
Let me do it again more slowly, this
is how it goes.

                    You tended
to slip off by yourself, would pretend
you'd died and come back as
a piece of string. Left over right
and under. It was while
you were down by the water
I perfected dragonfly bows
on your small and empty shoes.

Snail

Swirled around the secret that I keep at my core
I appear to be locked – and yet I can be opened
by the taste of rain;
$\qquad\qquad$ snug as a brain
in the chamber of the skull, harmless
as a cloud I float in a coil of quiet.

An ear that listens to the flavour of earth
you think I am slow – but I am already
where I need to be;
$\qquad\qquad$ if you love me
perhaps I'll uncurl on your hand
or write your name in silver on the roses.

Spider

When I throw it from the bedroom window
the spider is a black snowflake

the hairs on its body so delicate
they'd melt if you breathed on them.

The asterisk of its legs were a prayer
for safe landing: it was a mote

of darkness, an ink-blot to test
my sanity, the softly spoken name

I decide not to mention later
when I carry you over the threshold.

Woman in a Tank of Scorpions

Tonight we are not so curious –
familiar with the darkness behind your ear
the almond and vanilla of your navel,
we know the ways to travel: here
by the scar on your ankle
which took us so long to understand
I begin my overnight approach
to the hollow of hibiscus at your collar-bone.

Already the wing-nodes begin to swell
as we knew if we kept you safe
for seven nights they would. Perhaps
when the wedding is over, you'll dream
you were covered by butterflies:
turquoise and vermilion wings
which might, who knows, have lifted you
if only you'd waited.

The Night Before

Tomorrow, when birds with turquoise eyes
gather in trees whose flowers are drops of blood,
after a day of lizards and the yammer
of a creature in ecstasy or pain,
you'll discover the source of this river
and bathe in the pool beneath the waterfall
overhung with flowers you have yet to name.

Tonight, with my breeze against your lips,
you'll dream of being kissed, oblivious
to those grunts and rustlings, which may
or may not be friendly. Tomorrow will be
citrus and musk, mango and persimmon;
tonight I send you moths from the darkness,
words in a language you do not know.

Befriending the Shadow

I followed your advice – and when he called again
pressing on the window like an ocean
I lifted the catch and let him in:
he seemed a little younger than myself –
spare as a blade and gaunt
as a tree in winter, ice

in his eye and his grin bitten off
at the edges. On that first night
he prepared a meal from
feathers of blackbird, raven, crow;
a brackish stoup of rainwater
and seven peppermint stones

with a speckle of soot at the centre.
He shook out the words from my books
like the withered remains of spiders
and dipping the length of his arm
into a pool of mercury, recovered my image
from the bottom of the mirror.

Smiling and frowning, my face
flopped about like a dying fish –
he slipped it into place and it suited him.
He moved in his aquarium
with its charcoal minnow,
his collection of records

with fingerprint grooves
and bottles of ink like little
drops of darkness. He gathered
the corpses of beetles,
pinned them to the wall
like notes in a song,

painted with infinite care
each white key of the piano
alternately matt and gloss
and fell in love with my wife.
Tonight when she asked
Who's this stranger at the door?

he closed it in a final goodbye.
My key when I tried to use it
melted like a small black teardrop.
And now I am standing
on the wrong side of the pane
waiting for your next suggestion.

Pumice

I wish I were a stone
a mouse without a tail
at home by the taps and loofa.

You could chase me to the end
of your elbows, cat; I would
nibble at your heels.

My roughness is your reason
to be silky – my lightness
your occasion to sink.

Ignite yourself against me
softly – immerse yourself
in sunlight and marshmallow.

Hare

The bruise of your footprint lingered where
you stepped from the bath –
and I thought of the form of a hare
and how what made it lovely
was all it had released.

Here is the empty hand
you were holding only this morning,
I'll keep it by my side
to remember you.

The Boy Who Became a Table

Yes, I can tell you how it happened
how I turned the flat of my palms
towards each other, aligned my middle fingers
heard the vertebra snick into place
one by one. Today I am hoping to catch
the petals of seven roses,
to sleep without dreaming once.

As to why – it's harder to say:
but just last week she brought
chocolate and late-bottled harvest
for a midnight picnic together.
Should your time come, consider
how you will cope with spillages,
if sunlight will admire or corrode you,
could someone hide beneath you,
if they wanted?

Fathoming

To hide in a fish, you must slip
your fingers into the fin, forget
how to blink – soon you will breathe
by listening. Unable even to float,
at first I lost my equilibrium
constantly – I wanted to tickle
the surface, trailing a lazy dorsal.

Now, I am trying to decide
if the water tastes like starlight
or the smell of a peach. I am given
and taken by the under-swell,
I travel a season of dark. Now
I know I'm never coming out,
I may as well go deep.

Earthworm

Because I taught the blackbird
how to listen, this evening
I am nothing but a song.

The End of the Peninsula

1. Naming the Islands

From the end of your father's garden
ragged with nettles now
its fence overgrown with bittersweet,
the way back to his house is a voyage:
flower beds positioned on the lawn
reflect the arrangement of islands
off Fairhaven Bay.

Now you must name them in order:
Centaury, Vervain, Chesnut Bud, Beech –
as if you were entering harbour.
This was his way of showing you how
to come home. With the lighthouse
behind your shoulder, aligning
the spires of St Petrox and St Nons,
you learn to approach.

2. In Light Inaccessible

You woke with a shadow in your eyes
a blue and purple pool
which would not be dispelled by rubbing.
Moving round the kitchen on radar –
remembering a chair, holding hands
with a tap – you no longer need to see
in order to believe.

Wondering what happens next
you begin to feel invisible
almost as if you were an angel.
Perhaps in a moment or so
you'll walk through the wall of this house
and give your insubstance to the wind...
In the middle of all that exists
but cannot quite be seen
you close your eyes and smile.

3. The Snowdrop Girl

Even at a distance you know,
seeing her alone in the boat
she must have borrowed,
if asked – she would not tell.
And so for an hour or more
you watch her setting them adrift.

She holds them to her lips
for a moment, as if she were saying
to sprays of seventeen stems
in the waters of West Angle Bay:
Now you must learn to grow
where nothing has grown before.
After she's left you discover
as you make your way back to the house
you can't remember her face
or even what car she drove.

4. The Kitchen Table

In the end you remembered everything:
sealing wax, picture hook, sprig of asparagus,
removed one by one until
there was nothing left
and you saw all twelve quite clearly.

Now at his kitchen table
it seems you must start again
with packets of mustard stolen from cafés
a pair of Christmas cufflinks
shoes you wore as a child
wrapped up in newspaper under the sink
and the fox with an injured leg
seen in his garden the night before.
You look once again at the table
tasting each one with your mind
and soon you have them all
forever.

5. The Chinese Blackbird

Perhaps it's because there's no music
you find yourself humming one evening
towards the middle of April
as you watch the Chinese couple
who owned the Lucky Dragon
waltzing on the beach
quite slowly.

A blackbird is singing from a gorse bush
and it's only a matter of time
until they return to their bungalow.
Their feet are leaving ideograms
on the hard, wet sand. Either
they're letting the tide go out
or else they're bringing it in:
you can't make up your mind –
not being able to dance.

6. The End of the Peninsula

Things are quiet at the end of the peninsula –
nothing arrives but weather.
At dawn by the derelict lime-kiln
in a field of what may have been cabbages
silences wait to be populated
by the solitary figure of yourself.

You watch a petulant wind
shove the playground swings,
or stand by the fallen memorial
touching someone's name,
or walk on the beach in drizzle
chewing a popular song
as a notice appears on a tree
to tell you everything must go.

7. *Persephone*

The boat which is no more now
than seven sticks of wood on the beach
sails out to complete its journey
each year on the day of the disaster.

You won't refuse tonight
when your father invites you aboard:
the sea will be perfectly calm
and the stars overhead will listen
as he reads from *The Key to All Knowledge*
and shows you the illustrations
of unicorns, steam locomotives
and cities beneath the sea.

Shingle Street

A tide-bone of drift-wood
shivers in the desk light:
an ossified worm
licked by electricity.

One by one
the surrounding houses
douse their lights
and disappear.

The root-stem trembles:
a luminous blue dragonfly,
a needle which leans
to Orford and Ufford.

Night comes towards me
over the water,
the wind and waves
are breathing as one.

A wriggle of bone
from Shingle Street
is dancing
on my desk.

And here at last
looking through my window
is the quiet face
of the moon.

Dunce

November light
is frail.
A bulb left on all night
mistakenly, is pale

and barely conscious
in the overcast of day.
As one who's blundered into bliss
by way

of being wrong so often
and so well
it's good to see that orphan
burning calm and still.

Even

A spirit level
with my grandfather's name
beneath the bubble

holds its own
softly corrective
vowel of home.

A salve
of calm
to lave

the conundrum
of the mind,
it is plumb

as the blind
piano-tuner's ear,
trained to mend

what once was pure
and make it true
again with care.

Slow but sure
I ease the slippery oval
into view

and keep it level
out in the open
until the bubble

and I are even.

LOST

'Lost' implies a location, a geographical experience, possibly a landscape – there is a question inherent in the word. It also embodies the sense of some kind of emptying out, something not being there. It relates to memory and nostalgia and, at the same time, an oceanic freedom.

Tania Kovats

The art of losing isn't hard to master.

Elizabeth Bishop

i

The Missing Link

At the back of my ear
the mermaid's song
is a lullaby. At the back

of my eye the moon
is smooth as a bubble.
When rain-water freezes

on the hawthorn
I sleep beneath this wood.
Wrapped in a cloak

of butterfly wings
I dream of breathing water
and creatures without names

swimming at my shoulder
their voices in the darkness
calling me to follow.

ii

There Once was a Wood

You dream of hazels and hawthorns
in a corner of the kitchen, of a stream
that flows though our bed.

You hear a woodpecker throbbing:
the silence between his calls
a long held breath. You walk

downstairs and lay out a rug
in the garden: wood-avens
named for my family

spread beneath the trees;
the otters are pleased to see you,
the kingfisher comes to your hand.

iii

Ophelia's Letter to Virginia Woolf

You know the stones
as they come to hand:
each is a face

its eyelids closed
which speaks as soon
as you pick it up,

each is a word
on the river's tongue
which you must sound

as you go along.
You need their weight
to make you light

enough for death
to sing in the trees,
you need their weight

to let you walk
to the heart of where
there is no hurt.

One for the man
who will sit alone
to hear your voice

in an empty room
one for the shadow
across the lawn

and one for the lane
you must hurry along
as if you were terribly late.

iv

The Drowned Girl

A tiara of shells slips from your head.
A slick of hair curls around your ear
as you listen to the sky.

One of your arms is stretching out
as through reaching for a glass of water
the fingers of the other are folded over

closing the flower of your hand.
Letters in purple biro, circles
for the dot above each *i*

and a strip of passport photos
taken with a boy from nowhere
are waiting to be found.

Your head still flickers with jingles
and hymns: your mother's voice
your favourite song

but the scent of anemones and freesia
marzipan and mango tea
your passion for Arthur Rackham

and a jigsaw of Monet's garden
with three missing pieces
will not revive you. You do not

remember your name. Behind you
a stranger approaches, the wind
blows a bag along the beach.

v

The Visitor

When oranges and lemons
in the drowned conservatory
are candles through fog

and a heron fishes
the submerged streets
of the model village

I'll come to my senses
put on my skin
walk once again

through the flooded park:
my pockets full of elvers
swansdown in my hair

and a sodden bouquet
of gentians and camellias
soft in my arms

I'll make my way
to a house I know
and open the door –

my old umbrella
with folded sails
slowly unfurls

and murky puddles
of river water
spread from my feet

as I clear my throat
call your name
and wait.

vi

Wednesday

That night we were going to learn
to spell *abracadabra*. He knew
there were one seven six nought

yards in a mile. Sky-blue pink
with a yellow border was always
his favourite colour. He once

stood twelve three-penny bits
in a three-shilling ziggurat. Out
of the strong came forth sweetness

he told me that morning. Tonight
is the night I sleep in his bed and pretend
I've come home to myself.

vii

Leaves Around me Falling

Each year, on one particular morning
of heavy frost, our kitchen would still
be cold enough to show the brief

insubstance of my father's breath.
And then I knew it had come at last:
the morning when, as I walked to work,

all the trees along the way
would release their leaves.
Edged with frost they whispered

something I could not catch.
Returning home I used to dream
that each of the leaves could fall

into place on the tree again,
that each of the breaths my father broke
would keep him green.

viii

Fog

You wonder if the road will remember
how it's meant to go – if the beech tree
farm-yard and pub will be waiting

in their usual places. Your hands
on the wheel are a kind of prayer
to keep the fog from coming inside

and taking you away from yourself.
But where have the cross-roads got to?
And shouldn't that house with the slanted roof

have arrived by now? You're hoping
it isn't true – that story of the man
who emerged at a village

on the other side, and drove
to a house he seemed to know,
where a wife he'd never married

and children whose names
never crossed his tongue,
had waited all day for his return.

They sang him to sleep that night:
in the morning his car was a memory,
by evening he'd forgotten how to drive.

ix

Song

As if in the end
it were nothing more
than a broken saucer

instead of a car
with its wheels in the air
and someone lying down

by the side of the road
as if they didn't care
how they looked anymore,

the tinted plastic
and mirrored glass
have been swept away

and nothing's left
to mark the spot except
this robin singing.

x

Burnt-out Car

It showed how windows rose
and fell, how springs in the seats
were an hour-glass you squeezed to measure

how long you weighed. Pedals made it a piano:
music you sat inside of. A chrysalis
from which direction had escaped

it took you wherever you wanted
as clouds approached and passed
and sycamores kept their distance.

xi

Laika

These are my stars
I know their scent:
magnolia, blackthorn, peony –

nourished by a source
I do not understand
I chase my name

through the garden of heaven.
My origin is a nest
of roots and stems.

My body is molybdenum
and chlorophyll. My eyes
are petals of gold.

I am the dog-flower:
my bark is meadow-sweet
my blood is mercury.

Tasting the light
I blossom here
among my stars.

Icicles

Dribbles of rain and starlight
slowing to a stop by the down-spout,
starving themselves to nothing.

Overnight strangers who linger
where the gutter does not fit,
holding on one-handed.

As I child I trapped their drops:
crystal bees from a bitter hive
shivering on my tongue.

Slippery with brilliance
they wriggle their glinting tails:
platinum blonde Rapunzel

letting down her hair.
At first apart from a faint
but unmistakable tang

like aniseed or frankincense
you'd hardly know they were lit.
And then with a kind of whisper

the bones are feathered with flame:
a gentle, slender radiance –
buttercups and honey.

xiii

Lost

Toothbrush. Car keys. Wallet.
The number of someone
who seemed interested.

A ring that belonged to your mother
who found it in the street –
you put them down for a moment

and when you return they're gone:
as if in some mismanaged way
speaking in a language of absences

they were trying to tell you something.
It's almost like living in a fairy tale
where more and more the cursed princess

learns she must do with less and less:
her hair-brush and mirror, handsome prince,
the wish she was saving till last

which would let them live forever...
Death is forgetting where we've put ourselves
the moment when life gives up looking.

Prayer

Bring me the path
that leads through the gorse:
coconut and bee-song,

an upturned boat
where the butterflies sit,
the *Wherewithal*

riding at anchor.
Bring me the shade
of an over-grown well,

the smut-flies who wait
to be nipped from the air
by the likes of siskin,

yellow-hammer, twite:
zinc – zinc – zinc – zonk.
Bring me a choc-ice

to melt in my fingers,
the graunch of pebbles underfoot
and a woman

down by the tide-line
carefully gathering shells,
her spotted green pyjamas

rolled above her shins,
her hair tied up
by a strand of marram.

She will show me the grizzled beard
of an old yellow toothbrush
and the nest of the little tern,

she will show me herself as a lake:
her hands a pair of swans.
She will put the word *wife* in my mouth.

ACKNOWLEDGEMENTS

Acknowledgements are due to the editors of the following publications in which some of these poems, or versions of them, first appeared: *The Affectionate Punch, Brando's Hat, Breakfast All Day, Cascando, The Coffee-House, Critical Survey, The Frogmore Papers, The Honest Ulsterman, The Interpreter's House, The Magazine, The New Welsh Review, The North, Orbis, Poetry in the Waiting Room, Poetry London, Poetry Monthly, Prop, The Reater, The Rialto, The Shop, Smoke, Stand, Staple, Thumbscrew.*

The Library of Rain was runner-up in the Cardiff International Poetry Competition 1997. *The Storm Bell* was commissioned by Leicester City Council as part of the 'Words Out' Festival. *Teeth* won fourth prize in the Peterloo Open Poetry Competition 1998. *William Wordsworth's Socks* was commended in the Ways with Words/Faber & Faber Poetry Competition 1998.

Some of these poems first appeared in *The Storm Bell, William Wordsworth's Socks* and *Swarm Haugh Closes* published by The Hawthorn Press, Norfolk, with illustrations by Diane Byford.

Some of the poems from 'Lost' first appeared in *The Mermaid Room* published by Crocus Books, Manchester, which was a winner in the North West Poetry Pamphlet Competition 2000.

The quotation from Tania Kovats appeared in the 'Lost' exhibition leaflet, Ikon Gallery, Birmingham. The epigraph to *Swarm Haugh Closes* is taken from Christopher Bentley, *The Last True Englishman*, Gravesend Press, London, 1954.

Charles Bennett was born in 1954 and grew up in the North West of England. He started work at sixteen. At thirty he attended London University and was awarded a scholarship which allowed him to live in America for a year, where he studied with Joseph Brodsky. On his return he completed a doctorate in contemporary Irish poetry. Following a period as Head of English and Drama, he was appointed the Reader in Residence for Blackpool. Married, he lives and works in Ledbury, where he manages the poetry festival.